EASY TO MAKE

DRIED FLOWER

ARRANGING

MARY LAWRENCE

BROCKHAMPTON PRESS
LONDON

First published in Great Britain in 1994
by Anaya Publishers Ltd, Strode House,
44-50 Osnaburgh Street, London NW1 3ND

This edition published 1996 by Brockhampton Press,
a member of Hodder Headline PLC Group

Editor Samantha Gray
Design Watermark Communications Group Ltd
Photography Richard Paines
Illustrator Coral Mula

British Library Cataloguing in Publication Data

Lawrence, Mary
Easy to Make Dried Flowers
I. Title
745.92

ISBN 1-86019-149-5

Typeset by Servis Filmsetting Ltd, Manchester, UK
Colour reproduction by Scantrans Pte Ltd, Singapore
Printed and bound in EC

CONTENTS

Introduction

Arranging beautiful dried flowers, leaves and grasses together into exciting designs is one of the most pleasurable and rewarding of creative crafts and one that can be undertaken by everyone.

Arranging flowers is such a pleasurable and creative pastime. Dried flowers offer an inspirational range of shapes, colours and textures to be worked into exciting displays which will last for many months.

Dried flowers do not have the same constraints as fresh flowers and as a result allow the arranger far more flexibility. Dried flower heads can be used to decorate presents or to make delicate jewellery; leaves, grasses and lichen can be incorporated into stunning swags and wreaths which can be used time after time.

The fresh flowers are picked at the peak of their perfection and then carefully dried to preserve both their colours and shape. From the largest leaves, ferns and grasses to the smallest flowers, all can be used to create an infinite variety of designs.

This creative craft can be enjoyed at leisure all year round. As flowers bloom, and grasses ripen, gardens, hedgerows and even window-boxes will yield a constant supply of material for you to dry, and instructions on how to do this can be found in the Better Techniques section of this book.

Enthusiastic gardeners can grow their own favourite flowers especially for drying, and little space will be needed to

provide many months' supply. "Fair weather" gardeners who hesitate to venture out on cold, wet days can sit warm and snug indoors happily capturing the sights and scents of their garden as they prepare their dried flowers.

If you don't have a garden or prefer to have flowers that have been grown commercially, there is a better choice now than ever before. Flowers are grown and dried in England, France and Italy in ever increasing quantities, but Holland remains the world's centre for the industry. There they have researched flower drying and have made large investments in new methods for fast drying with temperature controlled air circulation in special rooms, so helping the flowers to keep their colour and shape. They also import exotic flowers from Africa, Australia, the Middle and Far East and South America for distribution throughout the world.

In this book I have used dried flowers to create some varied and more unusual designs that I hope you will find interesting and easy to make. I have listed the materials used, and the method and order in which I worked, but hope that I have left you the freedom to vary the materials and designs to suit your own particular ideas.

If you study my design approach, you will see how the elegant lines and the outlines flow to give the final shape to arrangements. I hope that you will see the balance and harmony in the proportions and find a new insight into the use of colour and texture.

Whether you are using this book as a beginner who will find the basic information enlightening, or as an experienced flower arranger who would like to try something different, it is my hope that you will share my sense of excitement and enjoyment when you are re-creating the designs.

So whatever the season, with this enjoyable hobby you will always be able to create an enchanting flower display.

ONE

Swags and Garlands

Wall Bow

One of the easiest ways to make an attractive wall display is with the clever use of paper ribbon. This original design also offers a very economic use of dried flowers.

Materials
4yds (3.6m) maroon paper ribbon
Foam posy bud
Reel wire
Glue stick (for glue gun)

Flowers
Pink rose buds *Rosa*
Copper beach leaves *Fagus sylvatica purpurea*
Broom bloom *Cytisus* (dyed pink, maroon)

Preparation
1 Divide the paper ribbon into two 2yd (1.8m) lengths.

2 Uncurl the paper ribbon and make three equal size loops, leaving one long end. Bind the loops tightly at the base with wire to secure. Cut off the ends of the wire, leaving about 8in (20cm) spare.

3 Repeat with the second length of paper ribbon.

4 Bind the two half bows together with wire to form the complete bow. Twist the ends of the two 8in (20cm) lengths of wire together to form a hanging ring.

5 Arrange the loops into an attractive shape. Cut a 'v' in the two ribbon ends. Secure the foam posy bud to the centre of the bow using wire or glue.

Design
6 Position a rose in the centre of the posy bud, then place the copper beach leaves to form an outer circle.

7 Wire small bunches of broom bloom and push into the foam around centre rose. Next position a circle of roses, then fill in the remaining gap with circles of alternate coloured broom bloom.

Bind the loops tightly at the base with reel wire.

Secure the foam posy bud to the centre of the completed paper bow.

Festive Wreath

A Christmas wreath that can be made in October is perfect for a busy person. This one is also pretty enough to display all the year round.

Materials
14in (35cm) foam wreath pad
12in (30cm) stub wires
Wire pins
Black reel wire
3yds (2.7m) wired edge ribbon 3in
  (7.5cm) wide

Flowers
Lichen (dyed green) *Cladonia*
Honesty seed heads *Lunaria annua*
Glixia (dyed red)
Poppy seed heads *Papaver orientalis*

Preparation
1 Push the 12in stub wire through the wreath and twist the ends together to form a hanging ring at the back.

2 Break the lichen into flat pieces.

Design
3 Pin the lichen to the inside edge of the wreath. Next pin lichen to the outside edge then fill in the centre.

Wire together groups of honesty seed heads.

4 Wire the shiny honesty seed heads into groups of five and trim the wires to leave two 3in (7.5cm) mounting legs. Repeat with the glixia, to make small bunches.

5 Position the bunches of honesty seed heads and glixia around the wreath, pushing the wires well into the foam. Intersperse the bunches with single poppy seed heads, pushed into the foam.

6 Cut a 42in (1.5m) piece of ribbon. Fold in half and secure from the middle, to the top of the wreath with wire.

7 Form the remaining ribbon into loops, held together at the base with reel wire. Attach to the top of the wreath with reel wire to make an attractive bow.

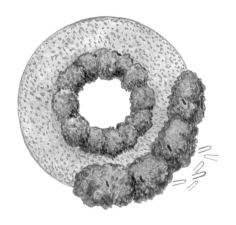

Pin lichen to inside and outside edge of wreath.

Bedroom Garland

This delightful garland of flowers on swathes of soft voile, hangs perfectly on a wall over a bed. Make it to whatever length you wish by changing the amount of voile used.

Materials
6½yds (5.8m) of 36in (90cm) wide voile fabric
Two 12in (30cm) stub wires
White stem tape
Silver reel wire
White cotton and needle
Glue stick (for glue gun)
Two hanging rings

Flowers and grasses
Yellow helichrysum *Helichrysum bracteatum*
Reed canary grass (dyed yellow)
Golden rod *Solidago virgaurea*
Eucalyptus *Eucalyptus gunnii*
Fescue grass

Preparation
1 Cut a length of voile 1½yds (1.3m) long. To neaten edges, turn under ¼in (6mm). Press and then turn under another ¼in (6mm). Press and secure with running stitches. Run gathering stitches along opposite ends of the voile. Gently draw up the thread to gather the fabric.

2 Cut the rest of the fabric into two 2½yds (2.6m) long strips. Neaten all the edges as above. Fold one piece of fabric into a three-loop bow, leaving two ends, one longer than the other. Secure with tiny stitches. Open out the voile loops to make a soft, large bow. Repeat with the other piece of fabric. Stitch a bow to each end of the centre swag, and a hanging ring to the back of each bow.

3 Make up small bunches of mixed flowers, grasses and foliage and secure with silver wire. Cover the two 12in (30cm) wires with white stem tape. Bend

one end of each of the wires into a hanging ring.

4 Using silver reel wire, attach bunches to the tape covered wires, starting at the

ring end. Overlap the bunches and cover stems and wire with stem tape as you proceed. Continue until there is 6in (15cm) of stub wire remaining. Fasten off the silver wire, covering with tape.

5 Make a second spray in the same way, and then overlap and join the two spray ends together. Cover the exposed 5in (12.5cm) of wire with stem tape.

6 Using glue to secure them, position the remaining flowers in the centre space, using the largest flower as a focal point. Make sure the stem tape is hidden.

7 Make two small bunches of mixed grasses. Stitch a bunch to each bow. Hang the garland over the centre swag and attach to the wall.

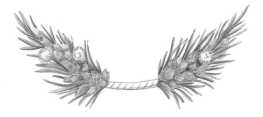

Overlap and join the two spray ends together.

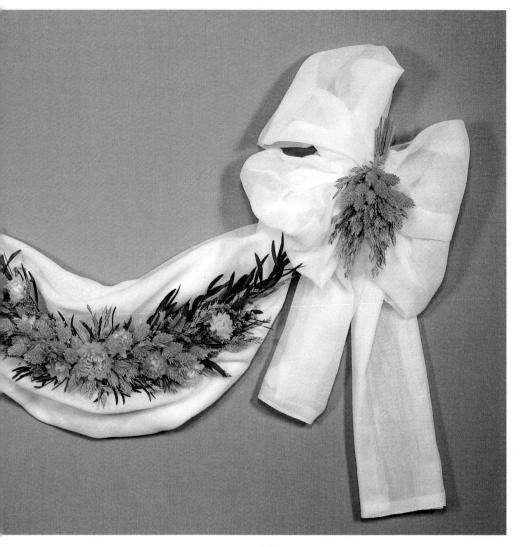

Kitchen Swag

Rough hessian and calico provide an excellent background for this rustic swag. The size of the arrangement can be varied to suit your kitchen.

Materials

Wire netting
Sphagnum moss
1yd (90cm) of 18in (45cm) wide hessian
1yd (90cm) of 4in (10cm) wide calico
Stub wires
Black reel wire
Glue stick (for glue gun)
Hanging ring

Dried Plant Material

Glycerined bracken and oak leaves
Barley and quaking grass
Lotus and poppy seed heads *Nelumbo lucifera, Papaver orientalis*
Mushroom and fungus
Globe artichokes *Cynara scolymus*
Sweet corn and chillies
Cinnamon sticks and apple slices

Preparation

1 Using wire netting and moss, make a garland base (see Better Techniques).

2 Glue the base to the centre of the hessian. Following the shape of the picture, gather and fold the fabric to the centre to form a soft rumpled effect. Use a glue gun to secure.

3 Fold the calico into a bow and attach a mounting wire to its centre.

4 Divide the small items into bunches, wire. Secure mounting wires to all the large single items (see Better Techniques).

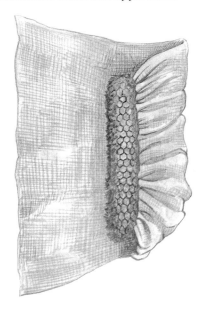

Place the garland base in the centre of the hessian and fold fabric into the centre.

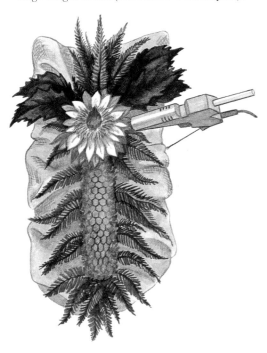

Stick the large artichoke to the top centre of the arrangement.

Design

5 Position the bracken to follow the line of the hessian.

6 Position a large flowering artichoke to the centre top and stick in place using a glue gun. This provides a focal point for the arrangement.

7 Starting at the base, arrange plant material to slope upwards and inwards towards the centre flower.

8 Attach a hanging ring to the back then place on a wall to view. Adjust as necessary, and finally position the calico bow.

17

Vine Wreath

This impressive wreath combines artificial fruits with dried grasses and flowers in a stylish display which is ideal for a dining room or hallway.

Materials
Vine wreath
Black reel wire
Maroon velvet ribbon
Stems of artificial fruits
Stems of artificial acorns
Glue stick (for glue gun)

Flowers
Oats *Avena fatua*
Peonies *Paeonia lactiflora*
Broom bloom (dyed maroon) *Cytisus*

Preparation

1 Wire the oats into bunches and stick on the wreath, forming a crescent shape.

2 Starting from the centre of the crescent shape, arrange sprays of artificial fruits and acorns to fan out on either side. Stick in position.

3 Group and secure the peonies in place with glue.

4 Make a large bow from the velvet ribbon and glue to the centre of the crescent allowing the ends to trail to the outer edges of the wreath.

5 Next wire broom bloom into bunches and position to fill in the gaps.

6 Group the discarded stems of oats into bunches and wire together. Position the stems to form a small crescent opposite the main design. Stick in place.

7 Trim the stem ends to make an attractive shape. Stick the fruits to the centre, and add broom bloom to complete the design.

Stick oat bunches onto the wreath to form a crescent shape.

Trim the stems into an attractive shape.

Taking care of arrangements

There are a few tips which should be followed to ensure any arrangement always looks as good as new.

Keep dried flowers out of direct sunlight as this will fade their colour. Try and avoid placing an arrangement over a hot radiator as the dry heat will often make the flowers brittle.

It is better to keep dried flowers out of bathrooms as they will absorb water from the atmosphere, become damp, and may become mildewed.

When an arrangement is finished, lightly spray it with hair lacquer or a special surface sealing product. This will help to minimise damage from knocks and bumps.

Keep cats or other pets away from the arrangement, to prevent them knocking and damaging the flowers.

Clean the dust off flowers with either a soft artist's brush, or using a hairdryer on the lowest setting, on a cool heat. The hairdryer should be held about 12in (30cm) from the flowers to allow the air to gently blow over the petals.

TWO

Table Decorations

Coffee Table

This attractive display is designed to be viewed from above to show off the full beauty of the conch shell, and is therefore perfect for a low coffee table.

Materials
Queen conch shell
Adhesive clay tape
Modelling clay
Black reel wire

Flowers
Dudinea *Dudinea*
Miniature roses *Rosa*
Campion seed heads (dyed pink)
Amaranthus
Achillea *Achillea*
Echinop (dyed pink) *Echinops*

Preparation
1 Press two strips of adhesive clay tape onto the inside of the shell.

2 Wedge a small ball of modelling clay onto the tape.

Design
3 Wire short bunches of dudinea, then position them on the outside edges of the modelling clay.

4 Fill in the centre of the display with wired bunches of roses.

5 Bunch and wire the seed heads. Position to imitate a shoal of fish swimming into the shell.

6 Group three soft stems of amarathus. Put at the base of the shell to resemble tentacles protruding out.

7 Fill in any remaining gaps with bunched achillea.

8 Finish by arranging the spikey echinop to peep out of the shell at the top.

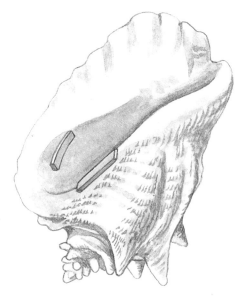

Stick adhesive clay tape to the inside of the shell.

Put the campion seed heads in place.

Hall Table

Placed on a hall table, the fresh perfume of this group of potted dried herbs and dramatic foliage display makes a perfect welcome for any visitor.

Materials
Glass tank
Plastic spike
Adhesive clay tape
Foam block
Miniature terracotta flower pots
Small foam ball
Latex adhesive
Wire pins

Plant material
Lichen *Cladonia*
Glycerined wattle
Glycerined eucalyptus *Eucalyptus gunnii*
Bay leaves *Laurus nobilis*
Thyme *Thymus vulgaris*
Marjoram *Origanum majorama*
Lavender *Lavendula officinalis*
Rosemary *Rosmarinus officinalis*

Preparation
1 Use clay tape to stick the plastic spike to the base of the tank.

2 Cut the foam to fit inside the tank leaving a 1in (2.5cm) gap all around. Push the foam onto the spike.

Cut the foam block down to size and then push it onto the spike.

3 Break some of the flower pots into large pieces. Turn the tank onto its side. Use a ruler to gently push lichen into the gap, adding an occasional pot or pot piece until the foam is covered.

4 Wedge small pieces of foam into four flower pots and cover with lichen.

Design
THE TANK
5 Begin to build up an outline by pushing the tall stems of fine foliage into the tank.

6 Position the large leaved foliage in centre front to form a strong focal point.

7 Fill in with the remaining foliage mixing the colours and allowing the stems to flow over the tank to give a soft, natural effect.

POTS OF HERBS
8 Cut dried herbs and lavender down to short stems. Arrange a herb in each pot, pushing the stems into the foam to form a small bush shape.

BAY BALL
9 Stroke along the underside centre vein of each bayleaf to encourage it to curl.

10 Take the foam ball and starting at the centre top, secure a row of leaves to the ball using latex adhesive.

Stroke the centre vein of each bayleaf to make it curl into shape.

11 Holding the top of the ball firmly in the palm of one hand, trim the lower ends of the leaves level. Secure the base of each leaf with a wire pin.

12 When dry, remove pins and stick a second row of leaves overlapping each of the first leaves. Make sure the tips of the leaves appear level all the way round the foam ball.

13 Repeat until the ball is covered in bay leaves. Fix the ball securely to the pot with clay tape.

Dressing Table

The dark wood of this miniature drawer unit makes a perfect setting for this resourceful design which uses up flower heads and broken stems to create a charming display.

Materials
Miniature drawer unit
Foam block
Black reel wire
Stem tape

Flowers
Blue larkspur *Delphinium consolida*
Sea lavender (dyed green) *Limonium*
Glixia (dyed red)
Glycerined bells of Ireland *Moluccella laevis*

Preparation
1 Cut foam and fill the top drawer. Leave the drawer open ¾in (1.8cm).

2 For the lower drawer cut the foam into a wedge shape then place it in the unit. Leave the drawer open 1½in (3.7cm).

3 Wire together bunches of larkspur flower heads. Push these into the foam in the top drawer.

4 Starting at the left of the top drawer, position the sea lavender to make an 'L' shape, carrying it through to the bottom drawer to fall over right corner.

5 Follow the same line with a few stems of larkspur, then with glixia.

6 Wire and tape single flowers of bells of Ireland, then position to give added depth to the arrangement.

7 Cover any exposed foam with sprigs of sea lavender.

Cut a foam wedge to fit snugly into each drawer. Replace drawers, leaving them slightly ajar.

Arrange larkspur in the top drawer, then make an 'L' shape with the sea lavender.

Table Centre

To be viewed from all angles, this Roman styled urn lends itself to this massed form of display so popular at the time of the court of the French King Louis XIV.

Materials
Large urn
Several blocks of foam
Wire mesh
Black reel wire
Stub wires
Canes

Flowers
Roses *Rosa*
Peonies *Paeonia lactiflora*
Helichrysum *Helichrysum bracteatum*
Broom bloom *Cytisus*
Celosia *Celosia*
Anaphalis *Anaphalis*
Poppy seed heads *Papaver orientalis*
Eucalyptus *Eucalyptus gunnii*

Preparation
1 Wedge several blocks of foam into the urn. Using a sharp knife fashion foam into a dome shape.

2 Cut a piece of mesh wire, then mould it over the foam. Bend under urn rim to secure. Great care must be taken to achieve a well balanced shape as the flowers will follow the line of this foundation.

Design
3 Divide all the light weight flowers into short bunches and bind with reel wire, leaving 3in (7.5cm) mounting legs.

4 Use stub wires to mount groups of roses and poppy seed heads. Use canes to mount the heavy celosia and peonies (see Better Techniques).

5 Following the dome shape, push the wired flowers into the foam.

6 Intersperse the groups with single flowers of peonies, roses, celosia and short stems of eucalyptus.

7 Finally, slowly turn urn to view and reposition flowers where necessary, to vary colour and texture until the required effect is achieved.

Following the dome shape, push the prepared flowers into the foam.

30

Dining Table

This candelabra decorated with dried flowers and grasses makes a stunning centrepiece that will be a talking point at any dinner party. The napkin sprays add that extra touch of elegance.

Materials

12in (30cm) stub wires
White stem tape
Silver reel wire
Candelabra
Glue stick (for glue gun)
24in (60cm) of 3in (7.5cm) wide wired
   edge ribbon

Flowers

Bleached hair grass
Eucalyptus *Eucalyptus gunnii*
African daisies *Arctotis stoechadifolia*
Cornflower *Centaurea cyanus*
Feverfew *Chrysanthemum parthenium*
Love-in-a-mist *Nigella damascena*
Cream helichrysum *Helichrysum
   bracteatum*
Ambrosinia *Ambrosinia*

Preparation

1 Cover stub wires with white stem tape
then bend into a circle. Next bend the
wire ends to form a hook and eye
fastener.

Bend the covered stub wires to form a circle.
Bend ends to form a hook and eye.

Design

2 Mount hair grass into 3in (7.5cm) long
bunches (see Better Techniques). Cover
wire with stem tape.

3 Mount 3in (7.5cm) pieces of eucalyptus
and cover wire with white stem tape.

4 Mount African daisies and cornflower
then make bunches of the feverfew, and
cover all wires with stem tape.

5 Use silver wire to bind the prepared
wired flowers to the stub wire circle.
Trim and conceal the ends with stem
tape.

6 Fasten the hook and eye, then place
the circle on top of one of the candle
bases on the candelabra.

7 Repeat stages 5 and 6 to make circlets
for the two remaining candle bases. Stick
single love-in-a-mist flowers to the hair
grass, forcing it to overhang.

Napkin Flowers

8 Spread hair grass into a 5in (12.5cm)
long spray and bind the end with stem
tape. Stick the cornflower heads and
love-in-a-mist on top of the grass with
glue. Place on a folded napkin.

9 Wire the helichrysum flower to the
short stems of ambrosinia then cover
with stem tape. Bend the ribbon into a
bow shape. Place the flowers in the centre
of the bow, then bind wire around the
ribbon to secure. Place on the napkin.

Wire and tape the prepared flowers to the stub
wire circles.

Christmas Table

This spectacular Christmas decoration is cleverly arranged on a cake stand so that the pedestal base will allow full use of valuable table space.

Materials
3in (7.5cm) wide candle and stand
Cake stand
Adhesive clay tape
Plastic securing spikes
Foam block
2yds (1.8m) of 3in (7.5cm) wide wired
  ribbon
Wire pins
Stub wires
Silver reel wire

Flowers
Eucalyptus leaves *Eucalyptus gunnii*
Amaranthus (dyed maroon) *Amaranthus*
Lichen (dyed maroon) *Cladonia*
Achillea (dyed maroon) *Achillea*
Cow parsley *Anthriscus sylvestris*
Safflower (dyed maroon) *Carthamus
  tinctorius*
Love-in-a-mist *Nigella damascena*

Preparation
1 Fix the candle to its stand and place in the centre of the cake stand.

2 Using adhesive clay tape, stick the plastic securing spikes around the candle.

3 Cut and shape the foam and impale it on the spikes to form a base for the arrangement.

4 Cut the ribbon into 10in (25cm) strips, fold and fix mounting wires to form a quantity of wired loops (see Better Techniques).

Design
5 Wire eucalyptus leaves into groups of three and position to stand up around the candle.

6 Position amaranthus and more leaves to lap over the edge of the plate.

Impale the shaped foam on the securing spikes.

Having arranged the eucalyptus leaves and amaranthus, pin lichen to the foam to cover the cake stand.

7 Pin the lichen to the foam to cover the plate. Next position the ribbon loops and shape to form a circle.

8 Push the achillea into the foam around the centre and in betweeen the bows.

Now wire the cow parsley into short bunches and position to highlight the achillea and to appear to tip over the edge of the plate. Finally use the remaining flowers to fill in any gaps in the arrangement.

37

THREE

Special Occasions

Child's Birthday

Inspire a child's imagination by creating a miniature dried garden for a birthday gift. The bonsai tree can be arranged in a single dish to make an ideal gift for Father's day.

Materials

Plastic securing spikes
Adhesive clay tape
Large meat plate
Foam blocks
Wire pins
Large rocks and small stones
Small figurine
Bonsai dish
Latex adhesive

Flowers and plant material

Bun (carpet) moss
Cornflowers *Centaurea cyanus*
Grasses
Wheat
Sorrel *Fumex acetosa*
Buttercups
Daisies
Feverfew *Tanacetum parthenium*
Berberis *Berberis*
Branch of twisted willow
Pressed lady's mantle flowers and small
   leaves *Alchemilla mollis*

Preparation

1 Using adhesive clay tape, stick several
spikes around the plate. Impale foam on
the spikes, shape to the plate and cut to
uneven heights with a sharp knife.

Design

2 Trim away the back of the bun moss,
and pin pieces to cover the plate, leaving
a gap at the back.

3 Push the made up tree (see below) into
the foam at the edge of the gap and then
place the rock to the left of the tree.

4 Position the cornflowers in the gap,
then continue placing more of them in
between the moss joins through the
centre, towards the edge of the plate.
Occasionally position a small stone, to
create the effect of a stream.

5 Place grasses, wheat and sorrel to
imitate trees. Position groups of flowers
in the moss joins and finally position a
child figurine at the pool's edge.

Bonsai Tree

1 Trim and clean the branch of twisted
willow to the required shape.

2 Wedge foam into the bonsai dish then
push the branch into the foam.

3 Using latex adhesive to secure, stick
pressed lady's mantle flowers and leaves
on some of the branches until the
required effect is obtained. Use tweezers
to pick up and position the lady's mantle.

4 Cover the base of the tree with a mixed
selection of stones.

Pin pieces of bun moss to the foam to cover the plate.

Using tweezers, stick pieces of lady's mantle to the branch.

42

Thank You Basket

This lovely basket makes a charming thank you gift. For an extra treat, you can fill the centre with fruit, sweets or fragrant pot pourri.

Materials

2yds (1.8m) of 3in (7.5cm) wide red loose weave ribbon

2yds (1.8m) of 3in (7.5cm) wide straw coloured ribbon

Black reel wire

Attractive handled basket

Glue stick (for glue gun)

Flowers

Glycerined bells of Ireland *Moluccella laevis*

Blue larkspur *Delphinium consolida*

Protea *Protea*

Celosia *Celosia*

Preparation

1 Make bows from each length of ribbon.

Design

2 Cut the bells of Ireland into short pieces above a node, and wire this circle of bracts to a small bunch of larkspur using reel wire to secure.

3 Glue these bunches at intervals around the rim of the basket.

4 Remove the stems from the protea and stick in position around the basket.

5 Break the celosia into small pieces and position to fill in the gaps around the basket rim.

6 Finally glue the bows in position, allowing the ends to sweep across the inside of the basket.

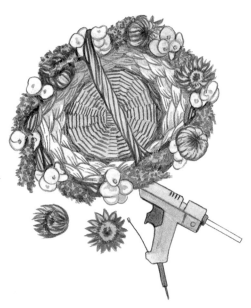

Add protea heads to the basket edge.

Wire together small bunches of bells of Ireland and larkspur, then glue around the basket rim.

44

A Valentine Tree

The time spent preparing this original gift will be rewarded by the spectacular finish achieved, and awed appreciation from the one you love.

Materials
8 × 1½in (20 × 3.7cm) branch
A triangular piece of wood size
   6 × 6 × 5in (15 × 15 × 12.5cm)
2½in (6.2cm) screw
Glue stick (for glue gun)
Block of foam
6in (15cm) diameter foam ball
Wire mesh
Stub wires
Black reel wire
Valentine ribbon

Flowers
Glycerined branches of broom (dyed
   green) *Cytisus*
70 red roses *Rosa*
Essential rose oil (optional)

Preparation
1 Trim and wire the broom into short bunches.

2 Cut 1 end of the branch into a point. Screw the flat end of the branch to the centre of the triangle to make the trunk. Stick bunches of broom to the edge of the triangle and trim to a height of 3in (7.5cm) then fill this base with foam.

3 Impale the foam ball onto the trunk and cover the foam with wire mesh, secured to the trunk.

4 Mount broom bunches onto stub wires.

Design
5 Starting at the top, push bunches into the foam. Keep turning the tree while adding bunches of broom until the foam is covered. Trim the tree to a good shape.

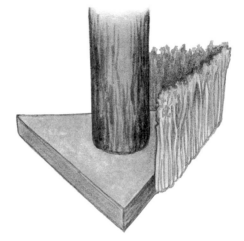

Glue bunches of broom to the edges of the wooden triangle.

Cover the foam ball with mesh and secure to the trunk.

46

6 Push some roses into the foam at the base of the tree. Perfume with essential rose oil if desired.

7 Mount more roses into variously sized groups and mount several singly. Position the roses in the foam ball in between the broom. Finish by tying ribbon around the base, and tying a bow at the front.

Mother's Day

This is the perfect day to give flowers to one who richly deserves them! This lovely arrangement will give pleasure long after Mother's special day.

Materials
Antique style basket with handle
Foam blocks
Wire pins
Artificial fruits
Stub wires

Flowers
Hydrangea *Hydrangea macrophylla*
Wattle (dyed maroon)
Roses *Rosa*
Pink larkspur *Delphinium consolida*
Achillea *Achillea*
Glycerined eucalyptus *Eucalyptus gunnii*

Preparation
1 Fill the basket with foam blocks.

Design
2 Break the hydrangea into small florets and pin to cover the edge of the foam.

3 Position wattle to form a fan outline.

4 Group the roses and mount onto sticks, and repeat with the artificial fruits.

5 Wire and mount the larkspur into bunches and repeat with the achillea.

6 Position the roses and fruit, placing some to extend over the front of the basket.

7 Break up the solidness by interspersing the spikey larkspur and eucalyptus.

Position the wattle to form a fan outline.

Cover the edge of the foam with hydrangea florets.

Silver Anniversary

A 25-year celebration requires a unique display. Palm leaves and bells of Ireland are transformed by the use of silver paint for this very special occasion.

Materials
Foam block
Tall, narrow white vase
Silver spray paint
Stub wires

Flowers
5 palm leaves (air dried)
4 glycerined stems of bells of Ireland
  Moluccella laevis

Preparation
1 Take the leaves and flowers to a spraying booth and give them several coats of silver paint. Care must be taken to lift and turn the bells of Ireland to make sure the bracts are completely covered.

2 Cut the foam to fit the vase allowing it to protrude above the top of the vase for about 1in (2.5cm).

Design
3 Position three palm leaves to form a soft outline.

4 Cut two palm leaves short and place at vase edge level.

5 Push three stems of bells of Ireland into the foam, allowing them to follow their own natural curves.

6 Cut short the remaining flowers and mount them to fill the centre front.

7 Wire together bunches of palm spikes and intersperse to break up the solidness of the arrangement.

First position the palm leaves.

Wire together bunches of palm spikes.

Retirement Picture

A retirement gift made with loving care will bring back happy memories, and when hung on the wall this original design will do just that.

Materials
Picture frame
Florist's foam
Florist's adhesive tape
Stub wires
Black reel wire

Flowers and Grasses
Lesser bulrush *Typha aryustifolia*
Reed grass
Protea *Protea*
Dryandra *Dryandra*
Bracts of corn on the cob
Fungus

Preparation
1 Cut a small block of foam and using adhesive tape, secure it to the bottom left corner of the picture frame.

Design
2 Position the bulrush to stand above the frame edge.

3 Place the remainder of the bulrush and grass, gradually working towards the centre.

4 Cut short the protea and dryandra and position them to make a cluster in the centre of the arrangement.

5 Mount the corn bracts and the dryandra foliage and intersperse throughout the design.

6 Cut and wire two pieces of fungus and position to break the frame line.

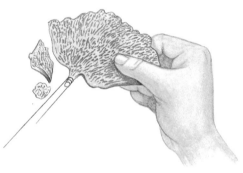

Wrap stub wire around the base of the fungus.

Position the reedmace to stand above the frame.

FOUR

Gifts and Accessories

Pretty Parcels

With a little time and effort, presents can be decorated to look very impressive by the novel use of a few pressed or dried flowers, arranged in an imaginative way.

Materials

Selection of small boxes
Coloured papers in green, black, pink, grey and blue
Selection of ribbons
Latex adhesive
Gold spray paint
Tweezers and tooth pick
Black reel wire
Stem tape
Glue stick (for glue gun)

Flowers

Hair grass
Pressed daisies
Blue larkspur *Delphinium consolida*
Grasses
Eucalyptus *Eucalyptus gunnii*
Maroon helichrysum *Helichrysum bracteatum*
Bleached broom bloom *Cytisus*
Honesty seed heads *Lunaria annua*
White anaphalis flower buds *Anaphalis*
Pink rose buds *Rosa*

Preparation

1 Wrap and tie ribbon to all parcels.

2 Spray the hair grass gold.

Designs

1 On the green parcel, pencil the number five. Using tweezers, pick up a daisy and place a small dot of latex adhesive on the underside. Position the daisy on the start of the pencil line. Repeat until pencil line is covered. Use $\frac{1}{2}$ sections of white petals on the vertical line.

2 Support the black drum on its side. Using the glue gun, stick short pieces of blue larkspur and grasses to make a pretty shape in the centre.

3 For the pink parcel, start by attaching the reel wire to a short stem of eucalyptus, then gradually bind in some helichrysum, broom and honesty seed heads. Trim the stems, tape the ends and then glue to the top of the parcel.

4 Pencil the figure 21 on the grey parcel then stick the white buds of anaphalis to the pencil lines with latex adhesive.

5 Place the last parcel on its side, then glue a rose bud in the centre. Encircle this flower with the remaining roses, held in place by glue. Intersperse the roses with short tufts of hair grass sprayed gold.

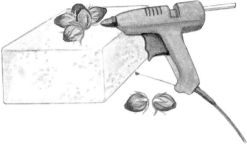

Make a circle of rosebuds around a central flower.

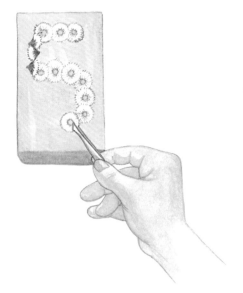

Stick the daisy heads along the pencil outline.

Lucky Horseshoe

Lucky heather and a well worn horseshoe, turned up, to catch good fortune would delight any happy couple on their wedding day.

Materials
Old horseshoe
Silver spray paint
White ribbon
Glue stick (for glue gun)

Flowers
Desiccant dried heather
Desiccant dried astrantia

Preparation
1 Scrub and dry the horseshoe. Take to a spray booth and give several coats of silver paint.

2 When the horseshoe is dry, form loops at each end of the ribbon then stick to the back of the horseshoe tips.

4 Stick flowers of astrantia to form a crescent shape on top of the heather.

Stick the heather to the bottom of the horseshoe in a reverse 'L' shape. Add the astrantia to finish.

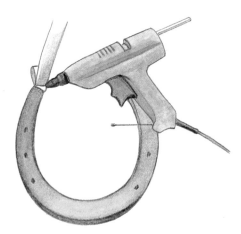

Stick the ribbon end to the back of the horseshoe tip.

Rose Confetti
Rose confetti is so easy to make. All that is required are large quantities of dried rose petals which can be perfumed with essential oil. They can be packed into drawstring bags made from white net to carry to the wedding.

Design
3 Lay heather in a reverse 'L' shape across the base of the horseshoe. Secure with glue from the glue gun.

Wheat Field Hat

Dried green wheat and red silk are combined to convert a plain black straw hat into a sophisticated accessory ready for a special occasion.

Materials
Red silk poppies
Black straw hat
30in (75cm) black petersham (corded silk
   ribbon)
Glue stick (for glue gun)
Black reel wire

Plant material
Stems of wheat

Preparation
1 Cut the stems away from the poppies.

2 Cut the wheat stems short, then wire the groups of discarded stems to make several bunches.

Design
3 Wrap the petersham around the base of the hat crown and pin in place. Hold up the poppy flowers and mark their required positions.

4 Remove the ribbon and stick the poppies in place on the ribbon.

5 Wrap the ribbon back around the hat and sew to the straw to secure in place.

6 Use the glue gun to stick heads of wheat to the petersham at the centre rim of the hat, then continue to position and secure the heads of wheat in a slanting direction around the rim until they meet at the back.

7 Make a short bunch of wheat then use the glue gun to stick the bunch to the centre of the hat.

Position and stick the wheat around the hat rim.

8 Glue bunches of stems in the centre to extend above the crown. Finally trim these stems into a fan shape.

Remove the ribbon from around the hat and stick the poppies to it.

Flower Jewellery

Dried flowers are a lovely material to make delicate pieces of jewellery with. Here fuchsia blooms and miniature roses make stunning earrings and a brooch.

Materials
2 silver ear wires
Silica gel
Spray varnish
Brooch bar
Glue stick (for glue gun)
2 silver ball and hook wires

Fresh flowers
Fuchsia blooms *Fuchsia*
Miniature rose flowers *Rosa*

Preparation
1 Choose perfect fuchsias from the plant, remove the ovary from the base of each flower, and carefully push a silver wire down into each flower.

Carefully push the wire down the centre of the fuchsia flower.

2 Gather perfect patio roses, cut the backs off the roses as close to the petals as possible.

3 With great care, transfer all these flowers to dry in the silica gel (see Better Techniques).

4 When the flowers are fully dry, remove them from the desiccant and gently remove every grain with a fine artist's brush.

5 Take the flowers to a spraying booth and very gently spray with varnish and leave to dry. Repeat this four times on all sides of the flowers. Hold the fuchsias so that the insides are completely covered.

Design
6 Push the brooch bar into a foam block so that it sits proud of the foam.

7 Glue the largest rose to the centre of the brooch bar. Next secure a smaller rose to either side of the centre one, holding each in position until the adhesive has set. Remove the brooch from the foam.

8 Using a pin, run a fine line of adhesive around the base of each fuchsia. Attach the silver ear wires to finish.

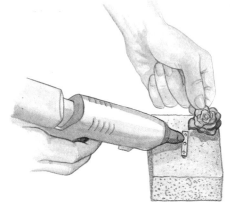

With the brooch bar held steady in a foam block, stick the flower heads in place.

Hair Combs and Slide

Beautiful accessories can be made for hair by using small flowers and grasses to decorate plain combs and slides. Choose a colour scheme to match an outfit.

Materials
Fine sandpaper
Selection of combs and slides
Glue stick (for glue gun)
Silver reel wire
Brown stem tape
Spray varnish

Flowers
Miniature Pink roses *Rosa*
Broom bloom (dyed maroon)
Eucalyptus leaves *Eucalyptus gunnii*
Canary grass heads
Blue larkspur florettes *Delphinium consolida*
Sandflower
Timothy grass
Dundinea

Preparation
1 Sandpaper the surface to be decorated, then wash and dry thoroughly.

Designs
1 **Hair comb** Trim away backs of roses. Arrange in line with the largest in the centre, graduating out to the smallest on the ends. Run a thick line of glue along the top edge of a comb and place each flower onto the glue in order. Fill in gaps with tiny pieces of broom.

Lay down a line of eucalyptus leaves along the top of the comb, then add four canary grass heads.

2 **Hair comb** Stick a line of eucalyptus leaves along the top of a comb. Position and secure four canary grass heads. Then take florets of larkspur and glue gun to form a cluster.

3 **Hair slide** Cut the sandflowers short then, using reel wire, bind three heads of Timothy grass together with dundinea. Continue binding the flowers to form a spray, while at the same time covering the wires with brown stem tape. Run a line of glue along the top of the slide and position the spray on the glue. Hold until set. Bend the surplus wire to the back of the slide.

Finishing
Place each of the articles into a paper bag, make a split to expose the flowers only. Take to a spray booth and give several sprays of varnish allowing them to dry between each coat.

Using reel wire, bind together a group of the flowers to form a spray.

Bridesmaid's Headdress

A bridesmaid's coronet made of dried flowers will look perfect for the whole of the day, and can be used after the wedding to make a memorable wall decoration.

Materials
Two 12in (30cm) stub wires
Silver reel wire
Brown stem tape
1½yds (1.35m) of 3in (7.5cm) wide
  maroon satin ribbon
Needle and maroon cotton

Flowers
Sorrel *Rumex acetosa*
Anaphalis (dyed pink) *Anaphalis*
White statice *Psylliostachys*
Achillea *Achillea*
Eucalyptus (dyed maroon) *Eucalyptus gunnii*
Hair grass (dyed maroon)

Preparation
1 Join the long wires together then cover with stem tape.

2 Measure this wire around the bridesmaid's head and bend ends to form a hook and eye join.

Design
3 Group the flowers together and wire together to make small mixed bunches. Tape the ends.

Gradually bind bunches to the head wire, taping to cover wire at the same time.

4 Begin the coronet by binding a bunch of flowers to the head wire.

5 Next gradually bind in other bunches, taping to cover the wire at the same time. Keep bending the head wire to avoid gaps developing while creating the coronet shape.

6 Finish by trimming and taping the end. Fasten hook and eye.

7 Form three loops in the centre of the length of ribbon, sew to secure. Attach the loops with glue to cover the join in the coronet. Trim ribbon ends to required length and cut each end into a 'v'.

Aromatic Posy

These old traditional European posies are fast gaining a revival as an antidote to the modern and ungreen ways of freshening a room.

Materials
Florist's bouquet handle
Lace posy frill
'Little egg' cowrie shells
2yds (1.8m) of 1in (2.5cm) wide ribbon
Glue stick (for glue gun)

Plant materials
Cedar cone
Cloves
Rosehips
Cardamom seeds
Beech masts
Cinnamon sticks
Fern leaves

Preparation
1 Position posy frill on handle

Design
2 Stick the cedar cone to the centre of the posy foam.

3 Position around the cone alternate cloves and shells, gluing to secure.

4 Next, push in a circle of rosehips.

5 Glue the next circle of alternate cardamom seeds and cloves.

6 Repeat a circle of rosehips followed by beech masts and an occasional stick of cinnamon.

7 Take individual leaflets of fern and position around the posy frill.

Finish with a circle of individual leaflets of fern.

8 Secure ribbon to the back of the posy and then stick cinnamon sticks to the trails to add a little extra spice.

Working out from the centre cedar cone, position a circle of alternate cloves and shells.

Better Techniques

&

This section gives advice on buying, drying, cleaning and storing dried flowers. It gives information on the equipment and techniques necessary to make this a most enjoyable craft.

DRIED FLOWERS
Buying
Commercial growers have invested heavily in drying equipment so that the flowers' vibrant colours are retained, and a tremendous variety are today available from florists, specialist shops and general stores.

Flowers When buying, care must be taken to check bunches are full size, wrapped in celophane and that the flowers are not brittle or broken.

Exotics This term covers the flowers, seed heads, cones and foliage imported into Europe from Africa, Asia, Australia and South America.

Fake dried These are a new type of polyester flowers, heated to give the fabric a shrivelled and 'dried' appearance. These will mix reasonably well in dried arrangements when the required dried flower is unavailable.

Artificial fruit The new styles are available on stems and when mixed with dried flowers can add texture and shape.

HOME DRYING METHODS
Gathering
Pick stems on a dry day as soon as the dew has dried off and the sap is rising. Flowers must be in optimum condition and preferably picked before pollination has taken place. If it is necessary to pick on a damp day, gently shake the flowers and stand them in a container in 1in (2.5cm) of water until they are dry.

Remember to pick grasses also, before they go to seed and pick seed heads before they rattle. Drying takes some time, so pick only as much as you can handle at one time.

PRESERVING METHODS
Air drying
Upside-down method Fix a line or pole across an airy, warm, dark room where the flowers can be left for some time. Strip all the foliage from the flowers, arrange bunches with their heads at various levels and secure the base of the stems with a rubber band. Using a strong stub wire, bend 'S' hooks and use these to hang the bunches, heads down, from the line or pole.

Do not have too many flowers in each bunch and leave room for the air to circulate between bunches. A darkened room helps retain the flowers' colours.

Hang bunches with heads down to dry.

Standing method Grasses, Chinese lanterns, sea lavender, statice and bulrushes are best dried in an upright position in a vase of dry sand. Lady's mantle and cow parsley should be started using the hanging method and, when nearly dry, transferred to a container so that they complete their drying in a more natural shape.

Support drying Heavy seed heads, like globe artichokes and sweet maize, need support and extra space while drying. Stretch a piece of wire netting over a wooden frame, put it in a warm place and place the stems through the wire mesh so that the netting supports the heads.

Support heavy seed heads with wire mesh.

Special treatments Hang large delphiniums and bells of Ireland stems singly. Helichrysums required for use as a single head should be wired after picking and before drying. Helichrysum dried on the stem, with some of the top foliage left on, can be gathered up into a simple but quickly made bunch arrangement.

Water drying
When hydrangea and yarrow start to become 'crisp' on the plant, pick them and bring them indoors to protect the flowers from the weather. Place the stems in a container of suitable height in 1in (2.5cm) of water. Allow to dry out in a cool place without adding more water.

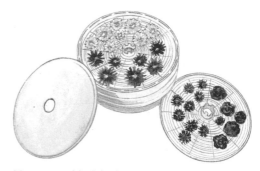

Use a vegetable dehydrator to dry small flowers.

De-humidifiers
Many homes now have room de-humidifiers and these are ideal for speeding up the drying time of larger batches of flowers in the hanging or standing method in a small darkened room. A vegetable dehydrator can in a day, dry batches of small whole flower stems or the heads of larger flowers (which can be given wire stems later).

Desiccants
There are four readily available substances which may be used as a desiccant:

Borax powder is perfect for fragile petals and can be dried and re-used but it is sometimes difficult to remove from the finer parts of the flowers.

Detergent powder will dry both small and large flowers but it should be used only once. Like borax, it can be difficult to remove from petals.

Silica gel This is the most expensive desiccant but it is the quickest and best one to use. It dries quickly and can be used with flowers of all sizes. Silica gel crystals can be ground down to a fine powder to dry even the smallest flowers, so they hold their shape.

Silver sand This works well with thicker petals and materials but it is slow-acting and can take up to three weeks. Also, it may not always remove the last traces of moisture.

Using desiccants

For this, you need a large tin or plastic box with an airtight lid. Place a layer of desiccant in the base of the box. Cut the flower stems short to ½in (1cm), sufficient to attach a wire after drying. Carefully lay the flowers in the desiccant, making sure that they do not touch. Using a spoon, slowly trickle desiccant among the petals and continue doing this until they are covered to a depth of about 1in (2.5cm). Seal on the lid.

Trickle silica gel from a spoon, separating the flower petals so that the crystals run between.

Inspect the flowers after a few days. They are ready when they are dry and feel papery. With silica gel, the process may take only 2–4 days.

If left too long, the flowers dry out and become too fragile to handle.

Carefully pour off the desiccant into another container and pick out the flowers, one at a time, as they come to the surface. Lay them on a plate or tray. Carefully brush any remaining desiccant from the petals with an artist's soft paint brush.

Turn the flowers upside down on soft, folded muslin and glue on false wire stems and then carefully cover the wire with stem tape.

Preserving with glycerine

Glycerine is mostly used for preserving foliage. It will change the colours of leaves to shades of brown but they will retain their suppleness. Unlike dried material, foliage preserved in this way is not easily damaged.

Stand branches in a jar of glycerine mixture, put the jar in a bucket.

Make up a mixture of 60% glycerine to 40% hot water. Pour the liquid into a glass jar and put the jar into a large container (such as a bucket). Strip the lower foliage from the branches and scrape the bark from the bottom 2in (5cm) of the stem. Crush the ends with a hammer and put the stems into the jar so that the bucket rim supports the branches.

Depending on the type of foliage, it will take between one and four weeks for the leaves to be preserved. You will be able to tell by the look and feel of the leaves when they are ready.

To preserve individual leaves, use a 50/50 mixture of glycerine and hot water. Place the leaves in a shallow dish and cover with the solution. Push the leaves down into the mixture from time to time. They should be ready in a few days. Lift out, wash in soapy water, spread on folded newspaper and pat dry.

SPECIALIST MATERIALS

Cones Pick these up under trees in winter or they can be obtained from some florist's suppliers and specialist shops. Kinds include cedar, Scots pine, larch and sugar pine.

Lichen In flower arranging this usually refers to reindeer moss from the arctic circle. The lichen is dyed and is useful for covering dry foam in arrangements.

Driftwood Pieces of suitable wood can sometimes be found on the seashore at low tide but driftwood is obtainable from florist's suppliers and specialist shops.

Fungus Sponge fungus and golden mushrooms have exciting shapes and textures and a wide range is usually available from florist's suppliers and specialist shops.

Gourds These can be grown from seed or you can buy them, ready-dried, from florists' suppliers.

Bun or carpet moss This is used to cover the surface of soil and gives a good finish to plant arrangements.

Twisted and tortured willow Useful and attractive bare branches which can be used in the natural state. Available from florist's suppliers and specialist shops.

TOOLS AND EQUIPMENT
Scissors
Florist's scissors are strong and intended for heavy work They will cut through hard stems, and wire.

Lightweight florist's scissors are light in the hand and sharp. Use them for cutting stems and ribbon.

Wire cutters are a useful extra and will help you to preserve your florist's scissors.

Stem strippers are useful for cleaning stems of thorns and foliage.

Adhesives
Hot melt glue gun This is the most effective way of securing dried flowers in place. The gun delivers the required amount of hot, liquid glue which quickly hardens as it sets.

Take great care when using this as the hot glue can cause nasty burns. Keep a bowl of cold water to hand in case of accidents.

Glue sticks For use in glue guns – these are packed in 5s, 10s or bulk in boxes, and are available in different setting times.

Latex adhesive is used to stick pressed flowers to paper or fabric.

Adhesive clay tape comes in a roll protected with a paper backing. It sticks firmly to glass and china and can be removed without damaging the surface.

Secured tape is semi-waterproof and is used to secure foam or wire netting to a container or base. It comes in two widths, ¼in and ½in (6mm and 12mm).

Stem tape is for covering wire. Stem tape is man-made and comes in pale and dark green, brown and white.

Plastic securing spikes
These are secured to glazed surfaces such as china or glass with adhesive clay tape. Florist's foam is then impaled on them.

Candle spikes
These fix into foam block and hold candles securely.

FLORIST'S MECHANICS
The term is used for anything which holds or supports flowers in an arrangement.

Dry florist's foam Is available in blocks that are easily cut to fit any container. It is also sold in several shapes including cones, balls, rings, posy holders and the smaller posy buds.

Wire netting Sometimes referred to as chicken wire, it comes in various mesh sizes but 2in (5cm) is best as it crumples easily and can be moulded without becoming too rigid.

Staysoft This is a trade name for a type of 'modelling clay' used to hold a small display of dried material.

Canes

A length of garden cane can be wired to heavy headed flowers and vegetables to support them and enable them to be mounted into foam.

Wires

Stub wires These are used to make false stems and for mounting flowers into foam. The most useful weight is 22 gauge and the useful lengths are 7in and 12in (17.5cm and 30cm).

Wire pins Are made by bending 5in (12.5cm) lengths of 22g wire in half and used for securing moss to foam.

Silver wires are for corsage and bouquet work. 28g is the most useful size and is available on a reel.

Reel wire is a fine, strong wire, sold on a reel and is used for bunching and binding. 'Blue annealed' wire looks black.

TECHNIQUES

Mounting wires
Attaching wires to flowers enables them to be secured to a base. Bind the wire round the stem leaving two 3in (7.5cm) 'legs' at the base.

Lightweight flowers which are to be inserted into foam can be wired with reel wire. Plant material which is to be mounted into moss bases requires black stub wire with one (or two) legs.

Gluing on a false stem
Place the flower face down. Wind the end of a stub wire three times around a nail to form a coil. Position the coil over the centre of the flower, covering any remaining stem, stick in place using a glue gun and hold in position until the glue is set.

Taping
This technique is used to conceal the wire of a false stem. Place the end of the stem tape behind the flower calix at a 45° angle. Tuck in the end and then twist the wired stem in the fingers while holding the stem tape taut. Continue twisting and taping, allowing the tape to creep down and cover the wire.

Pinning

This term is used when attaching stemless plant material to a moss or foam base with wire pins. Cut black stub wires into 5in (12.5cm) lengths, bend in half to form a two-pronged pin.

Mounting cones

Push one end of a 12in (30cm)-long No. 20 wire between the lowest scales of the cone leaving about 1½in (4cm) of the short end protruding. Tightly wind the wire around and through the cone scales to meet the short end. Twist the ends together to secure. Trim the short ends flush then bend the wire under the base. Use stem tape to conceal the wire.

Bunching dried flowers.

Spraying materials

Gold and silver spray paints can be used to change the appearance of cones, seed heads, twigs, etc.

Artist's gloss varnish adds an extra gleam to seed heads, gourds, dried fruits and vegetables.

Spray booth

This should always be used when spraying. Make one from a medium size rigid corrugated cardboard box which has a top with full flaps. Lay it on its side, and put in the item to be sprayed, and spray from about 12in (30cm) distance. Spraying is best done out of doors on a still day. It is advisable to use a disposable face-mask.

Bunching

This term describes the gathering together of flowers, shortening the stems and then binding them with black reel wire. Two 3in (7.5cm) wire 'legs' are left so that the flowers can then be mounted into foam.

Making a garland or wreath

Cut a piece of wire netting to the required length and to about 12in (30cm) wide. (If you are making a wreath, lay a circle of string to the diameter you want, then measure it.)

Lay the netting on a flat surface. Make a mound of damp sphagnum moss along the edge nearest to you. Roll the wire netting away from you and over the moss to form a roll. For a swag or garland, fold in the ends. For a wreath, bend the tube ends round until they touch, then 'sew' together with black reel wire. If the garland or wreath is to be used for dried material, leave it to dry before working on it.

Vine wreath

Use supple stems of vine or clematis. For an average sized wreath, cut stems to about 5ft (1.5m) long. Bend the strongest stem into a circle then secure the ends with reel wire. Now twine a second stem around the circle and secure with wire. Continue twining the stem around the orginal ring allowing their natural shape to leave holes and their tendrils to splay out, until the desired effect is achieved. Cut the wire then hang to dry and firm.

Ribbon bows

Form a length of ribbon into a figure-of-eight, holding the centre between thumb and forefinger. With a second length of ribbon make another figure-of-eight, holding the bows together at the centre. Bind the two bows together with a lightweight stub wire, leaving two mounting 'legs'. If you find making this method difficult, mount single loops and insert several in the same place.

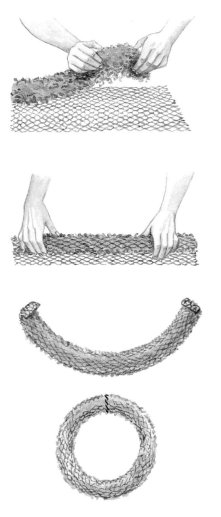

Paper bows
Untwist 3yd (2.75m) paper ribbon rope. Make a small 2in (5cm) loop and bind tightly with reel wire. Make a second loop, slightly larger, and bind again. Continue making loops of increasing size, binding each one tightly at the same position. Leave the last length of ribbon straight. Twist the reel wire ends together tightly leaving two 'legs'.

Cleaning dried arrangements
Clean dust from dried arrangements with a large, soft, artist's paintbrush or use a hair dryer at its lowest setting. Hold the dryer about 12in (30cm) away from the arrangement. Use the bowl of a wooden spoon to protect any fragile pieces.

Storage
Surplus dried flowers should be stored by rolling them in tissue paper and packing away in clean dry cardboard boxes in which holes have been punched. Flowers could sweat and grow mould if stored in plastic bags.

FLOWER AND PLANTS FOR DRYING

Air drying

Allium	Achillea
Agapanthus seed heads	Bamboo stems
Candytuft	Broom
Bells of Ireland	Cow parsley
Chinese lantern	Clary
Clematis seed heads	Cornflower
Dahlia (pompom)	Delphinium
Dock	Eucalyptus
Foxglove	Globe artichoke
Golden rod	Grasses
Gypsophila	Grape hyacinth seed heads
Heather	Helichrysum
Hogweed seed heads	Honesty
Hollyhock seed heads	Hops
Iris seed heads	Lady's mantle
Larkspur	Lavender
Love-in-a-mist seed heads	Moss
Montbretia	Love lies bleeding
Mimosa	Mugwort
Nipplewort	Pearly everlasting
Oats	Poppy seed heads
Sea holly	Sea lavender
Shepherd's purse	Sweet William
Statice	St John's wort
Sweetcorn heads	Tansy
Teasel seed heads	Wheat
Verbena	Veronica

Water drying

Bells of Ireland	Heather
Hydrangea	Yarrow
	Larkspur

Desiccant drying

Auricula	Anemone
Buttercup	Camellia
Cornflower	Carnation
Daffodil	Dahlia
Daisy	Delphinium
Elderflower	Forget-me-not
Freesia	Gentian
Geranium	Hellebore
Hollyhock	Lily of the valley
Marigold	Lily
Orchid	Peony
Pansy	Primrose
Ranuncula	Rose
Sweetpea	Violet
Zinnia	

Preserving in glycerine

Aspidistra	Beech
Bells of Ireland	Box
Broom	Bracken
Camellia	Choisya
Cotoneaster	Eucalyptus
Fatsia	Ferns
Ivy	Laurel
Laurustinus	Lime tree flowers
Magnolia	Mahonia
Oak	Old man's beard
Pittosporum	Rhododendron
Sea holly	Sweet chestnut

Useful addresses

Swan Craft Gallery
Ashfield cum Thorpe
Stowmarket, Suffolk, IP14 6LU
for floral materials, mechanics and
containers. Send a stamped, addressed
envelope for information and prices.

Lionheart Leisure Ltd
Elizabeth House
Queen Street
Abingdon OX14 3LN
for flower drying dehydrator kit.

Acknowledgements

Wedding dress used in photography
by Lynda Grey Designs, Crowfield,
Ipswich, Suffolk.